Sea-Level Zero

This book was supported by a grant
from the Eric Mathieu King Fund
of The Academy of American Poets

Sea-Level Zero

DANIELA CRĂSNARU

≈

Translated by Adam J. Sorkin
with the Poet

and with Sergiu Celac, Ioana Ieronim,
Mia Nazarie, and Maria-Ana Tupan

BOA Editions, Ltd. ≈ Rochester, NY ≈ 1999

LC #: 99–72450
ISBN: 1–880238–79–9 paper

First Edition
99 00 01 02   7 6 5 4 3 2 1

Publications by BOA Editions, Ltd.—
a not-for-profit corporation under section 501 (c) (3)
of the United States Internal Revenue Code—
are made possible with the assistance of grants from
the Literature Program of the New York State Council on the Arts,
the Literature Program of the National Endowment for the Arts,
the Lannan Foundation, the Sonia Raiziss Giop Charitable Foundation,
the Eric Mathieu King Fund of The Academy of American Poets,
The Halcyon Hill Foundation, as well as from
the Mary S. Mulligan Charitable Trust, the County of Monroe, NY,
Towers Perrin, and from many individual supporters, including
Richard Garth & Mimi Hwang, Judy & Dane Gordon, Robert & Willy Hursh,
and Pat & Michael Wilder.

Cover Design: Geri McCormick
Cover Art: "Woman in a Cloak" by Robert Marx.
Courtesy of Memorial Art Gallery of the University of Rochester,
Marion Stratton Gould Fund.
Typesetting: Richard Foerster
Manufacturing: McNaughton & Gunn, Lithographers
BOA Logo: Mirko

BOA Editions, Ltd.
Steven Huff, Publisher
Richard Garth, Chair, Board of Directors
A. Poulin, Jr., President & Founder (1976–1996)
260 East Avenue
Rochester, NY 14604

www.boaeditions.org

CONTENTS

II. Oxygen

III. Lethal Dose

IV. Seven Illusory Contours of America

V. The Writing Lesson

INTRODUCTION

Daniela Crăsnaru is one of the strongest and most celebrated voices in what for the last half of this century has been an exceptional, if underappreciated, poetic culture. Poetry in Romania, a small nation on the eastern margins of Europe as well as on the fringes of its Romance language group, can be compared in literary quality to the widely acclaimed poetry in English created at the opposite end of Europe in Ireland, an even smaller land which, likewise, lies on the periphery of its European language community. In either literary geography, a poet like Crăsnaru would stand out for her visceral power and lyric authenticity, her resigned yet transcendent irony and vivacious play of ideas.

Crăsnaru has been described repeatedly in terms reserved for the very best. She is nothing less than a "major" figure according to the published judgment of the eminent poet Ştefan Augustin Doinaş, a doyen of contemporary Romanian letters. Writing about Crăsnaru's 1988 selected poems, *The Window in the Wall*, when it won belated recognition in 1991 with the prestigious Romanian Academy Prize, Doinaş characterized the book as "the exceptional volume of an exceptional poet," despite its having been radically truncated by the fallen communist regime's censors. He went on to define Crăsnaru's dominant emphasis: "The general impression is that of confession articulated by an ego as plural being, in which, in fact, the deep identity is most significantly the unity of diversity, . . . the drama of . . . the redoubling of the personality."

Crăsnaru has herself spoken similarly of her subjective awareness of polarities within her makeup. In an interview on censorship, she remarked that her starting point was inevitably "a kind of inner duality" for which she suggested two pairs of phrases: "spirit and body," "lucidity and sensuality." The poetical works that result interweave Crăsnaru's impassioned rationality and a kind of spiritualized sense of the erotic in counterpoint to the ground bass that British translator Fleur Adcock heard as "an undercurrent of despair."

The drone of the repetitive nowhere of life's possibilities and eventualities, what the title poem calls "the sea-level zero of luck," serves poignantly to heighten the contrast of the frequently "insolent" physicality of the writer's textual garb, her always alluring "dress" of letters. In one sense Crăsnaru's inward psychological division may reflect the familiar situation of the not-so-simple separate person privately resistant to the tyranny of communist control. But at the same time the poems body themselves forth as the defiant protest of desire against mutability, loss, and limitation.

Not surprisingly, then, the act of poetry itself is central to the world of Crăsnaru's writing, the illusion of immortality through the continuity of print. In the phrase of another important Romanian critic, Nicolae Manolescu, Crăsnaru's poetry delineates "a spiritual predicament, which is one with the predicament of writing." This plight suffuses the poems' dramatized personal recognition of an antithesis between the warmth and passion of life in the flesh and life's inevitable betrayal in a kind of "letter-perfect" suicide, the elegant, jewel-like perfection of art imagined as a sort of stasis.

Crăsnaru's poetics, especially in the last two decades, is informed by a muted confessional method. Sylvia Plath, along with Anne Sexton, influenced a generation of important Romanian women poets who began their careers in the 1970s and who wound up relatively outspoken and morally engaged despite the nation's oppression. They were also less hermetic or solipsistic, less aesthetically oriented in the technical vocabulary and the interests of their writing, than most of the male authors of the decade, or the younger, self-advertised postmodernist poets of 1980s Romania.

For Crăsnaru, the quasi-confessional baring of the psyche can be associated directly with her apprehension of her impulse to generate poems as a kind of therapy. In her own analogy, literary creation is like "letting blood." As part of a discussion about how and why she writes, Crăsnaru explained to me, "When I'm overcharged with impressions and feelings, it's the most natural way to recover my balance." The reestablished poise of her emotional sensitivity is, among other things, an equilibrium of elements within the self, a catharsis expressed as the sounds, rhythms, images, lyrical persona, and discourse of poetry.

I first met Daniela Crăsnaru by chance in the summer of 1989, while I was in Romania on a Fulbright grant. I had recently translated some of her poems with Sergiu Celac. At the time, Crăsnaru and I had been—the only phrase for it—*not corresponding* for almost three years: most of our letters simply did not get through. Traveling in the north of the country on a carefully controlled, Romanian Writers' Union-sponsored excursion in commemoration of the hundredth anniversary of the death of the national poet, Mihai Eminescu, the group I was part of encountered Crăsnaru and fellow poet Grete Tartler in a hotel restaurant in Botoşani.

Though Crăsnaru and I were soon introduced, she and I could not talk, except for tense, well-intended blandishments. I easily sensed, and sympathized with, her unease. Crăsnaru had "retired" from her editing job for political reasons two years before and wasn't being permitted to publish. Moreover, she happened to be one of the poets whom I had already requested officially to meet, but I was getting stonewalled by Writers' Union protocol officials. During this awkward initial meeting, I was worried that, in the police state of 1980s Romania, the unauthorized contact of our crossing of paths in Botoşani, while clearly accidental, would produce additional problems for her.

When we met next in the summer of 1991, the December 1989 Romanian revolution fortunately had intervened. Crăsnaru and I could speak freely about her life, her work, and our mutual interests. I was by then firmly convinced that she was a compelling poet of deeply felt metaphorical power and careful formal composition. I knew I had to do further translations, which, back in Romania on an International Research and Exchange Board (IREX) grant, I commenced with the other native-speaking co-translators who had a hand in this book. I also managed to get together with Crăsnaru on a number of occasions and to interview her in her Bucharest apartment twice. One thing that startled me during our talks was Crăsnaru's use of purposeful craft not as merely an artistic matter but as her chosen strategy for keeping her artistic freedom inviolate.

As repression increased in Romania in the 1980s, Crăsnaru had begun intentionally to pack her lines with an abundance of figures and phrases as a mechanism for deceiving censorship. She would "write crowding, filling the page with very strong expressions to confuse *them*"—that always slightly stressed, indeterminate pronoun that no one ever misunderstood—"and force *them* not to be able to choose well." The result was a richness of texture that withstood political encroachments while it satisfied aesthetic imperatives. Crăsnaru is far from the only East European writer who discovered that censorship can serve inadvertently as a spur to invention and ingenuity.

It was when I saw Crăsnaru again during a week's trip to Romania in September 1992 that we committed ourselves to cooperation on a volume of her poems in English. She and I had each attended the first European Poetry Festival to be held in Sibiu, an ancient city just inside the arc of the Carpathian Mountains which form the natural boundary of Transylvania. Offhandedly, we discussed vague plans during the slow, uncomfortable train ride back to Bucharest, where we sat with Tess Gallagher, the other American at the festival, who was soon to work on poems by Liliana Ursu in translations with Ursu and myself. These brief, casual conversations became the germ of this collection.

A year later, Crăsnaru received an invitation to the University of Iowa International Writing Program. During her stay in the United States, we began translating her poems in tandem. Crăsnaru, who like her friend Grete Tartler had been well represented in the Oxford Poets series by Fleur Adcock, wanted to put her own hand on a new volume of her poems in English—to be entitled with the portmanteau place-name of "Austerloo," after the bittersweet poem that concludes the opening section of this book. The title soon changed, but our plans remained constant. Chiefly, Crăsnaru aimed for us to translate a body of fairly recent poems of hers not already in English and also newer poems she had written. Consequently, only seven works in *Sea-Level Zero* overlap with the previous book, *Letter from Darkness*.

The choices are primarily Crăsnaru's, with the omission of half a dozen other poems I had begun but, at her behest, abandoned. Forty-nine of the eighty poems in this volume are translated with the author, who has read over and approved the rest; more than two-thirds of the total translations were designed specifically for inclusion here. Most of the works previously published in Romania appear in Crăsnaru's 1987 book, *The Hemispheres of Magdeburg*. The order of the poems and their arrangement into five groupings are the poet's.

Both this collection and my friendship with Crăsnaru took a giant step forward in 1993 when, playing hooky from her Iowa regimen, Daniela twice stayed with my wife Nancy and me at our house in Havertown, Pennsylvania. Crăsnaru—whose English skills, obviously, are excellent— would give me her initial choices of English variants of her lines, with explanations, commentary, asides, hints at her intentions, citations of allusions, and possible alternative phrasing. I would scribble all of this half legibly on $8\frac{1}{2}$-by-11-inch, lined yellow pads, frantic to keep up. My pages quickly grew layered with comments and interpretations. In this way we prepared twenty new texts in that state that, perhaps because we were working in the kitchen, I thought of as "raw"—assembled heaps of ingredients for me to cook up in subsequent months, on my own.

I know that what Crăsnaru (jokingly, she has reassured me) claims to remember most about her stay is that, despite the cold weather, we kicked her outside to smoke and also that she did nothing but forced drudgery in poetry's kitchen. Nonetheless I seem to recall Daniela's delighting in the Halloween trick-or-treaters who came to the door and our wandering through enough of the nearby city of Philadelphia for her to write the final poem that made its way into this book, "The Streets of Philadelphia," completing the section of American poems five years later.

The majority of the poems in *Sea-Level Zero* derive from not only our collaboration in 1993 but also a heady, busy summer in 1995 when Crăsnaru and I were once more enabled to work together. Our month's labor took place amid the almost distractingly majestic surroundings of the Villa Serbelloni, the Rockefeller Foundation Study Center in Bellagio, Italy. The main part of our project during this residency was the translation of the first draft of a book of short stories culled from Crăsnaru's two volumes in Romanian, *The Grand Prize* (1983) and *The Fallen Cork Tree* (1990).

Our secondary but no less important purpose was to complete the manuscript of *Sea-Level Zero*. We went over my largely final versions of most of the poems translated two years earlier and roughed out eighteen more (three from both batches were left out of this book). In addition, she wrote nine poems for the collection in hand (a tenth we later agreed to cut). Most of her new poetry consisted of acerbic, bitingly sarcastic responses to the tensions and disappointments in her own life, especially the end of her marriage and its aftermath.

Of the Bellagio poems, five exist on paper solely in English, two in a mixed Romanian-English hybrid. Crăsnaru explained that working intensively in English and meandering through the town speaking Italian, it took too much mental energy to capture the poems in her native tongue. That is how she more or less conceived them, however. With four poems that she wrote down in Iowa in English, these were usually what caused us the greatest strain in our partnership.

This period in Italy most demanded and tried our trust. In the heat of translating, revising, polishing, and once again painstakingly revisiting poems, we found ourselves at friendly odds. Or worse! Sometimes we bickered over nouns like bargainers in a flea market, vied for verbs like children at a playground, wrangled about whatever frontsy-backsy we found to dispute in the disposition of poetic lines. I may seem to be exaggerating (and doubtless I am, a bit—even though the most minute choices are in no way inconsequential in poetry). Still, I cannot help but admit that one June day Daniela and I screamed at one another over contending synonyms, and on a bright morning we went so far as to argue, desperately and histrionically, definite versus indefinite article. Our fits of temper, of course, faded and passed like the ever-changing light over Lake Como. A few minutes or a few hours later, we climbed the hundreds of steps from the Gate House where we were housed to the sixteenth-century Lombard villa high on the steep, terraced hill for one of the usual elegant dinners, laughing at our squabbles along with my wife.

Some might be dismayed that we would call these poems for which there are no Romanian originals "translations." Yet, in the judgment of both the poet and myself, each one is indisputably a translation, despite the fact that I have in my files an exclusively, or predominantly, English draft in the poet's handwriting (or, for the Iowa poems, a typed copy Crăsnaru mailed me before returning to Romania in 1993). If a translation, you may scoff, translation from what? Well, from an ideal, unwritten original, just as in many theories of poetry, whether inspired utterance or the crafted artifact of genius, the literary work is in actuality a pale, secondary version of some Platonic form of primary poem.

With a half-cynical nod to current technospeak, I tend to think of the result as "virtual translation." When Crăsnaru and I talked over one of these drafts, it was clear to me the Romanian original was right there, perhaps barely out of reach in her head. But she could, and often did, grab on to it. Frequently while consulting about the poems, I appealed to her with "What's the Romanian for that?" whenever I needed clarification of a statement or perhaps an expedient, tactful basis for suggesting modifications. And once in a while I found I could resolve dilemmas over these English-language crystallizations of the poet's imagination with, "Well, sometimes I've translated that word (or that phrase) as. . . ." For, although I'm not fluent in Romanian, I've absorbed more than enough of the lexicon to have had a running mental tape of possible terms that might approximate the English we were tinkering with.

Through this most intimate of translation processes, a deeply co-creative one in which we equally surrendered ourselves to the higher duty of rendering a conceptual original, some of the poems you have here are effectively ghost-translations, manifestations of something that isn't. The eleven translated poems without source-language originals are the residue of a trace, like those photographs of fleeting subatomic particles of whose theoretical existence the photo is ocular proof, the visible presence of an absence, the sign of an idea. This book of Daniela Crăsnaru's poetry in English may wind up being the only verbal incarnation these poems ever have.

AJS

A NOTE ON PRONUNCIATION

This book retains a few characters from the Romanian alphabet not found in English (i.e., English letters with diacritical marks), which are pronounced as follows:

â	=	short *i*, as in "w*i*n"
ă	=	short *a*, as in "*a*lone"
ç or Ç	=	*sh*, as in "ru*sh*"
ţ or Ţ	=	*ts*, as in "ea*ts*"

I. Austerloo

SUNSET BOULEVARD

How my youth has flown, under every sort of flag:
faded hopes, trivial questions,
placating dialogues! In delicate mannerist poems,
where melancholy no longer distresses a soul.
How gifted she is, how circumspect, this chubby little girl
who must never, never, never grow
into adolescence! Plastic flowers as a boutonniere
for this fragment of life stored with such care on the shelves.
Then the small revolt, a waft of naive hope, of oxygen.
My impatience to speak of certain things
by name. But "What's in a name? That which we call a rose
by any other word would smell as sweet."
And so it goes. A whiff of darkness on the down escalator
to the basement of memory, the automaton who has usurped my place
to search through the dictionary of neologisms for more suitable
        sentiments.
With monstrous hypodermics of rainwater I would have cured
the leukemia of this highway of nightfall. At its end
the poem through which I breathe lies in wait,
a dead-tired, cyanotic lung in which I cast molten lead.

How my youth has flown. Straight from the young-hopefuls' squad
to the old-boys' team, my wheezing sadness scarcely able to put on
        its jersey
for the neighborhood recreation leagues.
"Six pastoral poems in a row equals six square yards of nature"—
        so they said.
Fiction, this commodious hammock. Through its mesh, as if between
        bars,
heaven inspects what happens here on earth.
Then irony, a last chance, the fiery glove with which I kept on trying
to defuse the fat-bellied grenade bulging with all that can happen.
The blast, its hellish roar. The immense crater—an eye socket

into which, someday, with his boots,
God will stamp down the rest of the prospects.

A. J. S.

INDIGO, VIOLET

In the horse's belly
the Greeks guzzle wine and get set
for victory.
On the day before the final day
the Trojans have no idea
that tomorrow is the final day.
The Thirty Years' War, too,
is in the thirtieth year.
On the penultimate day
of its thirtieth year
the soldiers likewise have no idea
that tomorrow is the final day.
The Hundred Years' War
is in the ninety-ninth year.
On the final day
of its ninety-ninth year
not one of the soldiers has any idea
that today is the final day
although
the odor of death is discernible
from a thousand leagues off,
the odor of death
as close to the odor of love
as violet to indigo
in light's spectrum.

Before your heart
a sundial of stone,
a minute hand
that all too soon
will turn to stone.

Indigo, violet:
the odor of love and the odor of death,

a pair of butterflies
twinned in a clay chrysalis.

Before your heart
a sundial of stone, a minute hand
stone still.

Not today, not today—maybe *tomorrow*,
the word contorted in a final spasm
snaking from the corner of clenched lips.
Tomorrow.
Dye of purple, thin dribble of blood
beneath the perfect mask of the Pharaoh.

A. J. S.

THE BULLET

He is a pronoun.
He is the third person.
Between myself and me
is he.
A bitter bullet
which neither I nor me
could have calibrated to
the barrel of this perfect weapon
from which the unrelenting void explodes
in gales of laughter.
And that's why we resist. We hadn't
the courage.
With our four hands hacked off
snuffling on the scent of its glassy arc.
With four blind eyes beholding it,
we, the desperate pronoun
of my double solitude.
With our single heart
which didn't know how to receive it.
That's why we resist. We hadn't
the courage.

He is a pronoun.
The third person.
He is, he could have been
Persona, Corona, or maybe
God Himself
who could truly free
myself from me.

A. J. S. & D. C.

THE LAST DAY OF POMPEII

In the entrails of the sacrificed birds,
in the volcano's hieroglyphics of smoke,
the word *extinction* could have been divined.
The inhabitants of Pompeii were forewarned.
Not one of them would believe it.
I know—I believe: This embrace
could be the last.
No, it's not the fear invading my cells
but my nausea before this army of jaded tourists
photographing the petrified lava,
pain's grimace, a sort of commerce with death
from which just that, death, is missing.
The ashes, behind which
are only
ashes.
The words, behind which—
other words.

A. J. S. & D. C.

THE MONSTER

I don't have a memory. I've labored hard
for that.
I've used my claws and teeth to dig out
every instant gone by
from the carcass still pulsing with blood.
I've nothing that ever happened.
All the happenings that were mine
belong to others now.
I out-live. I'm looking behind me
and my look engenders where I've gone
pillars of salt and mountains of tears
turned to stone.

A. J. S. & I. I.

CLASSIC MOVIES

About the private life of the stuntman
nothing is known.
How happy he was
as stand-in for the principal actor
as the fall guy who died instead of
the deathless hero.
Lights. Camera. Kiss.
A car lost in the night. He
and she at the hotel in C——
in a hot shower. Scraps
from the royal repast. Sequences
pirated from the archive
with the sharp money as surety.
The resurrection of myths. In the foreground
a close-up of Adam rooting out
rib after rib in slow motion,
an army of Eves superintending
his heart disclosed to everyone's eyes—his two-cycle
heart like a Trabant
chugging up a hill without traffic signs.
Lights. Camera. Kiss.
In the background what slapdash disarray
what a crush of extras
their chests pressed to the objective lens
to get themselves noticed
for even the walk-ons to be seen. What a huge
objective, how they race toward it
trampling underfoot all those
about whom in the credits it's written
"and others."
Ribbon rosettes fusillades of fireworks wolf-whistles.
Admiring, of course. As hard-pressed as at
hard-rock concerts hard times.
The diligent student reads

the recommended reading list.
Ginger Rogers and Fred Astaire
step by step *pas de deux* on the screen
until the final screening of the world
until the storyboard's happy ending.
Oh, and the words, what fiery
words. Playback.
The apathetic seducer dubbing himself
in the studio fondling a warm
demitasse of coffee reading from the scenario syllable by syllable
immeasurably bored: *dorogaia moia*
mon amour szerelmem
Tape it again, shouts the director,
with more sincerity, more passion.
My dear sir, don't you see how she suffers.
Turn it up a notch. We need your peak, the pitch
of your role this afternoon:
mon amour honey honey
dorogaia moia.
Now when the silent movie could still be very good
with its ridiculous sped-up gestures
with its between-the-wars perfume
with its gales of contagious laughter
over the tears rotting on the cheek
I long for the fight with whipped cream,
a real sequence for
a ton of cream a kilogram
a gram.
Now when there's unexposed footage left to shoot
when the stuntman hasn't hurtled down
from the skyscraper when
the director the coach the animal tamer
has yet to call out: Action!
Lights. Camera. Kiss.

A. J. S. & D. C.

THE WINDOW IN THE WALL

Along the wall and flush against blankness
with hands stretched wide with face glued to it
breath returning into the nostrils
infused with moist darkness
one step one day another step another day
here is where it should be
exactly here the window really *is*
the rectangle of gray.

With chalk-covered hands I caress its frame
as though I were caressing your shoulders your thighs
what operatic light might pour in from outside
what an uproar of scorching sap.
And what else might I devise in your absence:
a downpour in mocking torrents an English park
through which bound with enormous leaps
the hunting hounds
the sky gray flagstone
supported by my own breath
a hill in the background
ignoring all the rules of classical perspective
a golgotha of lead
overgrown with interjections, moaned and diminutive?
And what else might lie outside this window
that I don't have the courage to break through
that I can never open at all
this window clumsily sketched
by my hand roughly chalked
here on the wall?

A. J. S. & M.-A. T

CHESHIRE CAT

A row of sparkling vowels
like the teeth of a movie star
your smile
speaks of near nothing
a substitute
a sentence without consonants
a complex sentence of yours
about yourself.
A substitute for a sketch.
Underneath, in the depths, in the viscera,
in the occipital lobe, in the balloon's gondola of blindness
nuclear storms, capillaries in explosion
words and happenings.
Nothing can be seen here in this conventional
light.
Not even your lips.
Only the smile. That much:
a clause of fear.

A. J. S. & M. N.

LETTER TO NEMO

No one can experience
what he can't describe.
Fragments of jazz, joints squeezed in the hand
minor themes and variations.
Surfaces and surfaces.
A happy grammar of the trivial
orders all his events.
Life in a low, white room high above the city—
the fixed balloon-gondola, driftless.
Samples of life on shelves
books from those who ran the risk of living
before description. Samples of blood.
He can speak about descriptions,
nothing about blood.
The bee walled in the hexagonal cell
exudes image of honey having in memory
image of acacia
from a thousand years ago.
Dead imagination, imagine the fragrance.

He can't experience what he can't describe.
About the polyhedral iris of death
drowsing in still young cells
he knows nothing.
He can't describe it, not even traversing
the twenty thousand leagues beneath his deathless
blood.

A. J. S. & I. I.

EFFICIENCY, ECSTASY

The table, the glass that's full, the friends. fewer, ever fewer.
yesterday just like today. then surely tomorrow. then it's not too late
to give up. this very modest dose of
cyanide which your spirit secretes, will that do it?
efficiency. ecstasy. 24-carat tears. a definition
(like a manifesto between the prison bars)—
animus anima.

A. J. S.

POCKET SURVIVAL MANUAL

1. Things to forget:
      The desire of being desired.
      The thought of being thought of.
      The dream of still being dreamt about.

2. Remedies:
      Press both hands to your eyes.
      Begin to like this darkness.
      Begin to feel its purity, its melodic infinitude.
      Gradually accustom yourself to the other darkness,
         from down below.

A. J. S. & D. C.

FAUN, ANGEL

The kernel. upon the dome of your mouth. sugary pomegranate
in the imagination. acid-bitter
reality of this afternoon. faun. angel.
such disillusion. what disillusion?
crude sketch of an elaborate drawing. tomorrow, later, or maybe now
the anamorphosis.

A. J. S.

CONTEST IMAGE

A busload of blind
tourists
making an around-the-world tour
click click their cameras flash
focused on reality
oh, says the reality
this fat little girl
delicately clutching the hem of her skirt
curtsying gracefully
oh, repeats the jury of the unseeing
in this planetary contest
for cartoons
a prize for an image
which doesn't exist
it's OK it's great it's super

A. J. S. & D. C.

THE PAINTING

After a painting by Ion Gheorghiu

On the white wall, where my insomnia used to draw
endless corridors in flame, the blood mixed with the chalky white
of a flower crushed in memory,
on an oh so ordinary autumn afternoon
they hammered nails, they found twine, and there they hung
the painting. A painting lent as a kind of gift for a number of days,
a number of seasons, a number of feelings.
Lent, like the wall itself, like my child and my life,
like everything I possess, lent like these words
for which I'll never be able to pay the true price.
Thus I began to write the poem "The Painting."

Late in the evening, I went to look at it
and it seemed to me that I heard the little key turning in the music box
I'd sorely wanted but couldn't ever have.
Plink-plink, the only music I could readily
slice my veins on, *plink-plink,* blood oozing
along the arm, mixed with ink
on this white page which until yesterday used to be the wall.
I might have suspected a conspiracy of autumn,
of the imagination, of all those dear to me, if I hadn't sensed,
quite plainly, the perfume of the murderous lilies,
if I hadn't felt the acute necessity to come closer and closer
to it, to its movement of carnivorous and sensual shapes,
as in childhood I'd felt the necessity to bring my hand closer and closer
to the blue flame of the gas burner or the blades of the fan.
Rough brown, black and green, small interstices
with a thin thread of blood trickling through. *Plink-plink,*
if I could simply find the strength to turn away and leave
while I still have time, to turn back from this consequence,
from this poem which with no chance of my escape is luring me

straight into the cyclone of the blades, into the black flame,
into the core.

What is the theme of this poem, this
brief musical fragment, this painting?
I'll be expelled. I'll lose a year, I'll lose all the years.
Tell me I haven't understood anything in the slightest.
He, who right now is turning the small key of the music box
as tight as it can turn,
he, who knows so well that death is a frenzied
adolescent girl, a rose in flames with a bitter savor,
swirling on his meninges in pirouette, in arabesque.
I wanted to write the poem "The Painting" and I couldn't
because I still inhabit this borrowed body of mine,
because I still breathe, I who possess nothing,
I who no longer possess even myself,
because I haven't been asked to redeem for blood—
the sole price I'd be ready to pay in debt—
my hand that yet lives, my hand that yet writes,
devoured by the letters of the holy alphabet.

A. J. S. & D. C.

POINT OF CONVERGENCE

Waiting for the essential convergence—a sign, perhaps, a word
to change the equilibrium of light, a landscape to absorb
the darkness seething in the cells, a man—a pretext
for some lines to help me cross the roiling water
of a July afternoon
when
the time through which I'm passing isn't mine, with its sad,
clownish acrobatics—let it go, forget it, it's such an effort
to put the defense mechanisms into working order, nothing
can touch me, nothing can touch me, nothing.
My body through which I'm passing, it belongs to me less and less,
illicitly crisscrossed by small, vital spasms,
its melancholy flesh a purely lexical invention.
Again, the telephone call didn't come
it won't come
that street doesn't exist anymore
this time Halley's comet failed to reach
the earth.
With the feeling that you've missed by just a little bit, that you'll
miss again by just that little bit, still waiting for
the essential convergence,
through some mistake inhabiting another body and another time
inhabiting a mistake, a mismeasured inch, an unticked second
an evanescent feeling, another word than that very one
which could help you change the equilibrium of light.
In a drawer (of memory?), a pen from the town of Bitterburg,
a plastic tote bag with the slogan "Bet on Bitterburg":
a bit of memory, a bet on love,
a bitter memory, a bettor's destiny,
a betrayal—but no etymological connection with bitterness,
the local historians say.
And again from the acute angle of cold
where words themselves cannot cure me anymore
now in this endless second

when this poem, too, playing me false, has changed its trajectory
evading the bull's-eye, the explosion, the sign
which this time hasn't at all appeared
which I know is never to appear—the point of convergence
between my words' life, and mine.

A. J. S. & D. C.

THE THIRTY-YEAR-OLD BODY

I've stopped struggling against you,
neurotic cage.
I've drawn up the bridge.
I've recalled my ambassadors.
In vain you send bored emissaries,
merchants of illusion.
All deals are off.
I have no more (I am no more) than a tiny incandescent crystal
which nonetheless will be the Lion's share.
And the Lion, yes, the Lion himself will come. Much too soon.
But his sovereign claw
won't deign to honor you by crushing you.
For thirty years, my fears
like a legion of the blind
across your astonished thresholds.
For thirty years, my spirit
a corporal making a forced march upon your glorious ashes and dust
bearing a pack of words on its back.
Enough of that. The shamelessness of your good luck,
your glittering misery,
will no longer see
a single syllable out of me.
For thirty years, polishing my bars,
then to end up loving them,
multiplying them geometrically.

A. J. S.

EULOGY FOR APRIL

1.

I supposed I was cured of you, April epilepsy, but I wasn't.
The lewd tips of the buds moistening the air, the clamor of chlorophyll
    in the roots,
the whirlpool of colors.
How my dead body twitches between the anode and cathode
    of these scents,
this landscape. My dead body which dies once again,
remembering.
Between anode and cathode, stabbed as far as the core, my memory
    charged
into recovery. And *she* comes, the adolescent from more than twenty
    years ago,
with her fiery thighs, provocative, scourging the air,
her moist purple flower shedding light. Oh! how I hate her
before I kill her.
I'm afraid of you, April epilepsy, of your artificial lung
forcing me to inhale this air that drives me out of my mind!
Afraid of the throbbing network of pipes that keep me alive.

2.

On an April morning, at 8:15 A.M., I viewed my brain:
a bouquet of red flowers on the chest in the living room. From the cold
    of the petals,
from the frightful glow radiating everywhere around it, I knew
    what it was.
With both my hands I plunged into its matter, in a fury I plunged
until my palms felt the fiery paste swallowing
my arms, drowning me in myself, at last setting me free
for a few fleeting moments,

curing me of my April epilepsy, this continuous and indecent spasm like love and death, which are indecent exactly because of their sheer perfection.

A. J. S. & D. C.

I'M SO AFRAID OF YOU, BEAUTY, IMMENSE SACK

silvery cement-mixer.
Loving you, I'm afraid of you,
leather pouch smelling of nubile skin, of sap,
of divine purity.

In your entrails I saw heaped together
the grass, the phosphorescent rot,
the night's chimeras and words, every sort of occurrence.
Human blood.
All this and much more, too,
gorging the glowing viscera,
immense purse with insatiably opened strings.

Now as I write,
I'm staring into your depths with fear and humility,
your cement-mixer churning the planets of this life.

On the asphalt in the glare of noon I observe
a student's blotter. Written on it in reverse:
me, me, me. A pronoun crushed under the feet of passersby,
under all the world's grime.

Even this image enters into your immense belly,
Beauty, wholly given over to tears.
Love and crime, memory with all its armies
lost in the vast expanses of ice.
The worm burrowing through the apple's cellars,
yes, and my hand putrefying in the curvature
of the ideal letter.

That's why I'm afraid of you, loving you,
that's why I'm afraid of you as I write
with your chain tucked beneath my collar
now when I'm happily skipping about,

with your image around my neck like a millstone,
in the whirlpool where the words
may someday smell
of divine purity
of human blood.

A. J. S. & D. C.

MOLE UNDER THE SKULL

As if almost nothing can ever really happen,
I'm waiting for morning.
The juggler's hoop falls *clang*
around my docile neck. Right in place.
Oh, thank you very much. And you?
My eviscerated words
go on polishing the adverbial: of place and of time.
At the appointed hour,
more neutral than Switzerland,
my gestures, my pulse, my sight.

Night after night, she leads me into her underground,
the icy mole.

What do you see there? Tell me at once, tell me
everything that you see, she insists, shoving me
deeper and deeper, digging new tunnels
with the cut tongue of my words,
with my scream in whose placenta
dwells memory.

A. J. S. & D. C.

AFTER THE FALL

As if after the fall of the great empires, an endless exhaustion of the
    fiber, of the nerves,
of matter itself. Millions of worms, like bundles of light rays,
pouring out from under the makeup, invading new territories. The sea
    at flood,
one immense wave inundating the deserted beach, that place
you wanted to believe is now free, but no, it isn't—pure and pristine,
    but it isn't.
Everything is different. Without asking yourself how and why, like a
    blind man who once every ten years
feels his face all over, fingers recomposing another mask,
fingers touching another firmness of his skin, other wrinkles.
Everything different. On the epidermis of things, on the known face of
    the moon.
And here, down in the depths, in the core of the ever bitterer flesh, in
    the aorta's crook,
in the blood-swollen bulb of the heart, all is the same.
My freedom gets called loneliness. That's it. And beyond, an
    anonymous chorus,
shattering its echo on the disquieted threshold of each day. And
    beyond,
tons more makeup, myriads more harness bells. Anecdotes, topsy-turvy
    ideograms
which I no longer have time to decipher.
Imprisoned here, down in the depths, in an ever denser darkness of
    flesh,
speaking to his black star as I'd speak to a lover, not from outside
but inside myself, as I'd speak to my own last end,
with barely a trace in the flesh left by the knife,
a hint of salt on the cheek left by a tear.
Squatting in this cube, this tumbling die, only I am here,
feeling at home, only he, this cellular darkness all mine, all mine.
And beyond that, I have nothing, need nothing.

With my eyes shut, with my fingers sliced off, I restore landscapes from
    memory, from touch,
my own body devoured by the lead termites of words.
With my eyes shut, with my fingers sliced off, with wings of ice.

A. J. S. & D. C.

HIDDEN HEART

In the attic of some rented emotions
an adolescent in the shell of ever bitterer flesh
absurd pearl surrounded by darkness, by the sneering laughter
of the blind who are learning by ear
the art of description.
On this screen the network of nerves becomes visible,
the skein of blood,
and even the heart becomes visible,
the inaudible heart.

The Polaroid of the tourist in Tyrolean lederhosen
    yodel-lay-hee-ay-hee-yodel-lay-hee
is in instantaneous ecstasy *wie schön, wie schön*
tzuika aha, mamaligutza.
The tourist's Polaroid sees nothing, understands
nothing.
White on white, *qu'ils sont gentils les roumains!*
oh, such a pleasure, *drug moi.*
While you weld words with an acetylene torch
of tears trying to explicate more convincingly the adverbials
of place and time. And the archaisms:
"*Haraci*, in plural *haraciuri*, noun neuter (obs.). Annual tribute
paid the Ottoman Empire by countries in vassalage.
One of the four quarterly installments [fr. Turk. *harac*]."
Through the curtain of fat of the ears, nothing penetrates.
The Polaroid focuses on a comely Romanian lass,
the young waitress with picture-postcard sex appeal holding out smiles
    and garlic sausages.

As though you've been descending by elevator from the roof
    of the world,
you experience emptiness in the pit of your stomach as you confront
    this network of high-tension lines,
of untranslatable phrases, of emotions which seem to have meaning

in the Romanian language alone.
You, with your paltry words, your painful love,
here, on these streets in this city you love
precisely the way it is, as you love your sick child, flushed with fever,
carbonized angel, copy of a naive hope, the future perfect tense,
your sick child whom you love better than your healthy child
and whom you won't ever, ever, ever abandon.

Furiously you tear up the pictures in the adolescent's room,
posters of brightly colored airports, sensual flowers from Hawaii
which protrude their tongues at you, immaculate lawns
on which a white ball echoes *thunk-thunk*
in the rhythm of your pulse,
in the rhythm of the drop which keeps falling, falling on the crown
     of your head—
and your scream sweeps away the trains speeding toward the sea
shattering the windows of this second with cotton candy, confetti,
impish pucks of gasoline.
This second, a scrawny Trojan horse
from which your words will clamber down—manikin clowns
in gingerbread armor, in marzipan.
Let me gaze and gaze at this flayed wall,
on which the many-colored patterns keep forming cave paintings,
a geography of the incredible.
This wall set free. A screen
on which the network of nerves becomes visible,
the skein of blood, of sweat, of flowing tears.
Even the heart.

A. J. S. & D. C.

JULY

Let there be a cool and austere room
where you're waiting
for nothing, wanting nothing,
in a cone of light, in a lapidary stillness
like in the paintings of the Dutch masters.
But here it's a July street
where you're walking as if in sleep
under heavy, dusty-green treetops, swaying,
feverish, sensual.
Don't stop, you tell yourself, pretend you don't understand,
wish for a cold frosted window
you can press your hot body against
until your every cell
assumes the temperature of the frozen crystal
behind the bones of your forehead.
Don't stop, you tell yourself, walking as if in sleep
on this July street
the exact way you've been walking for such a long time
on the back stairs of all the happenings that are yours,
with your heart ready to explode from your chest,
absurd pearl captive in the shell
of ever bitterer flesh.
Of course it's hard, because it's
the middle of the day, of the year,
of your body,
stranger and stranger every moment.
". . . And next, *the body*."
Through an open window somewhere on the ground floor,
you hear the voice of a teacher of Romanian grammar.
"*The body*," repeats the student, "*trupul*, noun neuter,
neuter, neuter, in the accusative."
"Go on," you hear the teacher say, "don't stop."
"We have"—the student's tremulous voice is liquefied
by the afternoon, molten and fiery—

"further we have the noun *iubire: love,*
singular, feminine, nominative,
from the secondary vocabulary . . . "

A. J. S. & D. C.

THE MATCHBOX AND OTHER THINGS

That was the day when I began to hate objects.
Sad, skinny little girl, for hours and hours looking
from my first-floor window—staring outside, but
in fact into the courtyard of the building.
My eyes follow a small matchbox tumbling down,
reaching the earth. In a few minutes, footsteps on the stairs,
the fat, white-haired man picking it up
and lighting a cigarette.
Suddenly I remember Valentin
falling down the stairwell at our kindergarten.
The immense pool of blood spreading on the ground.
Stay away! Don't touch him! The useless white car
with a red cross and then his mother's black scarf
—the same colors as the matchbox.
That was the day when I began to hate objects.
The matchbox was the first.
My parents' desperate efforts to buy a new carpet
and a few other things; their obsessive desire for a washing machine.
Hating objects makes my life easier.
I can fly. I float free. I live in the gondola of a balloon,
tossing overboard objects whose life is longer
than mine, lofting higher and higher.
But all the same, from here above,
I continue to see the carpet in my
father's bedroom,
ten years after his death.

A. J. S. & D. C.

THE REHEARSAL STAGE

The coolness, the half-light.
We are resuming. Refining our action.
The very same action.
Its obscure corpse
abandoned under a swarm of devouring words.
The director calls out, Run through it once again.
Take it from there, from hatred. No, from there, from tenderness,
from there, from hesitation.
Reach within, hold on, breathe deep!
Come close to the chalk mark
to the center, to the core
from which true gestures can spring, will spring forth
the genuine attitudes for which we have
so great a need.
Sure, sure, you have the right to choose between a pirouette
and a curtsy, between going on your knees
and crawling, between collapse and flight.
Just be more natural!
For Christ's sake, try to imagine
that over there's the water, and farther on, the skirt of the forest,
that merely a little more is left, about three speeches,
and a saving hand will haul you up by the hair,
will eventually pluck you out
of that whirlpool swirling ceaselessly.
Close your eyes. That's it. . .

Imagine that the wind is blowing softly, softly,
that you're home, that you're ten,
that your mother and your father are alive
so very youthful and so very happy
and only now are you to make that central speech
which sustains the entire scaffolding,
this entire classical action of this classical text
which we haven't any means of changing

not through lighting, not through scenery, not through direction.
There's no choice here after all. Is this clear to you?
If so, then let's resume.
From despair. No. From confusion. No, no.
From the beginning.

A. J. S. & M.-A. T.

ÉCORCHÉ

I who made my success.
I who made everyone disappointed.
I who could not make me
hate myself on the day
he met me.
I me mine my—
entirely with memory, entirely with what's gone by.
Oh,
I have more and more difficulty making shift with myself.
I'm more and more disgusted with myself.
I who can no longer make out in any word
the pseudonym of God.

A. J. S.

THE PERFECT EYE

Nothing about the twilight of the flesh, about
the wave of disgust smothering you.
You study your hand as if some alien thing,
a skittish animal that, instead of you,
touches the things your eye
perceives another way.
Between all and everything, another kind
of distance. You haven't the least notion
how this distance can be measured. Nor why.
Your quivering hand, or your eye turned within itself,
or your endless nightmare from last night
now goes about drawing
the landscape you're bound to enter.
With a painful precision, detail after detail,
under the huge lens of an endless tear.
With the feeling you belong less and less to yourself,
you try to pretend
that near the edge
of the frame you've already entered
you don't notice that tiny spot you must reach:
the target.
Up a steep road, a narrow street,
a stairway without steps.
At its end, ribbons in her hair,
death, this obscene little girl:
uncovering her knees, spreading
her legs wide apart, staring at you
with that moist, treacherous, seductive eye.

A. J. S. & D. C.

AUSTERLOO

Both his critics and his fans well know
where the General lost and where he carried the day.
Every resident of Saint Helena knows, too,
what was at Austerlitz and what had to be at Waterloo.

Only I, I always confused
the defeat with the victory,
the battlefields, the balance of forces,
the pennants and the enemy.
And this isn't the simple case
of a student who was left back and made a mercenary
for frivolous posterity. All my victories
turn out defeats.
All the plunder captured by my army of words
marching disoriented
through an endless Siberia of doubt
has proved to be fed to bursting with my own blood.
Even "the odor of death as close to the odor of love
as violet to indigo in light's spectrum."

With my crack divisions cut down by half,
my years gorging the humus of this sheet of paper.
With my sharpshooters
crushed between the covers of my books.

My hand writing this battlefield log without a clue
as to whether it's alive
or dead.
June 14, Austerloo.

A. J. S. & D. C.

II. Oxygen

FAIRY TALE IN FRAGMENTS

O, Hänsel, welche Not!

1.

M from memory—melancholy's minutia, marsupium
which I rest in, crushed by celestial juices
milk-sapped poppy, murderous belladonna, mandragora.
therapy of the great astral conjunction
Mars the red, in magnificence
M a trident
thrust smack in the middle
while I am here, inside balloons of helium
on chlorine streets, in mercury rooms.
sprinkle some more millet, scatter some more flour oh,
soror mea mors
how shall we ever find our way back?
we've lost our way in a wood of fell signs, of fellow creatures,
with a thousand gingerbread cottages
he-he, ha-ha, give me your finger through the bars
give me this frail poem
that does not gain enough weight
light the oven, its blazing red sizzle—
books burn, words don't.

2.

M from magic. metalanguage. how are you doing = I love you
in an unknown language.
memory, lightning flash that reveals
horrible fissures, gaping faults. out of them
incubi arise to encircle you
with their demonic hoots of laughter
even now when

birds and hideous beasts and water sprinklers
have effaced all the traces we scattered.
it's all for the good, why should we ever make our way back
yes, it's better here
in the melodious darkness
in the devouring fire that has no memory.

3.

Mild mollusk, meek snail.
day in day out.
fairy tale in fragments, in smithereens
impossible to reconstruct. the dust
at the bottom of the drawing
almost outside the frame
a stalk of myosotis beheaded.
eyes don't see it. don't recognize it and feel no pain.
on the deserted and antiseptic white streets death doles out
boxes of toy letters for children.

A. J. S. & M. N.

THE RAFT OF THE *MEDUSA*

*You should pity the hermaphrodite
species for their twinned, thus their
doubly entwined, solitude.*
　　　　—Domokos Szilágyi

1.

Down in the depths, in the interior waters below.
From far far away can be seen the light
of the icy crystal.
But from up close? Capillaries throbbing,
nerves rearing up. Vermin of life.
Shipwrecked here down in the depths
in the interior cosmos, ambivalent
masculine feminine together in one, and I also with my
osmotic melancholy.
The ah of pain, the ah of pleasure.
The black water lily but also its stem
the frenetic eel
and also the river through which are coursing
the viscera spread open for the festival
and the living struggle that fills them too.
Everything, everything here
nothing beyond, in the delusive light,
its hullabaloo.

2.

Solitude in the interior waters. It's for no one
I am waiting
because no one's there beyond, except for me
in this interior cosmos permeated
by my own image.
Oh, how I hate this place where I feel so good

as I've never felt there beyond
in the physical landscape
as I've never felt by the side of my child
nor in the arms of any man.
Oh, how I hate this place where I feel so good.

3.

No one but you, love, who have no name,
only for your body is there no room left
here on this raft of death.
My androgynous spirit
within whose placenta words are pulsing
no longer has need of you.
The ah of pain, the ah of pleasure—
no   more   can   I
no, no more do I want to return
no more to flee from here
from this white rectangle of paper
on which I drift floating *in aeternum*
with myself dead in my own arms
Pietà Rondanini.

4.

I have needed many many years to discover
that no one's there beyond, waiting for me.
Year after year have I toiled
on this floating rectangle.
Year after year
have I nourished Imagination
this wild beast which swallows me
each and every time I show fear.

A. J. S. & I. I.

OXYGEN

1.

A cloud like a strangling lock from Fate's hair
sight takes it in, the eye soaks it up
beneath consciousness.
High above, a lid, above
the roof of the world
among every kind of rock-hard risk
eye and hand don't heed you
solely your shining little demon
the quartz crystal
a lamp burning
in the voluptuous dark.

2.

Letters. Letters which need something from you, from your life
from your air
to roof over this skullcap of ice
this abstract peak
this white surface on which your traces are
letters, letters, letters.
No wolves come to pick up their scent, to tear them to pieces,
only your own future
thrown behind you
as if you were journeying to face with the past.

3.

"I'm so afraid," I say in the second's nitrogen
which suffocates me.
"You're putting on airs," they tell me, opening the cock for chlorine

mimicking a mother's tones, illustrating scenes from my childhood
with watercolors—
my retina, my auricle and stapes
still react perfectly.
Down, get on the tips of your toes,
keep to your knees.
That's it. An anaerobic plant:
gather, put everything off, wait.

4.

Shallow breaths, one after another heavier and heavier
the sweaty verge of tears.
Life in the capillaries—a tumultuous marketplace
the merchants in the temple, oh.
Gall of grief.

Each word a birthmark
on the flame it arose from.

Smudged with ink as if with alien blood
this thought which writes no more than itself.

5.

In the frame of a book jacket,
in the casement of an open window, on its sill
like a character in Tolstoy
I
in the sizzle of a red dress
my body aloof, insolent.
A satisfying image.
Down below, far lower, a rabble of people and dogs.
Yells, firemen, nets spread wide.
No, no, that's not it!
Let it burn.

A satisfying image.
But I've never had
a red dress.
And I live on the ground floor
feet always firmly grounded.

6.

With fading strength, up, right up to it,
under the strangling lock of the cloud
almost no air, almost no respiration.

To be driven in flames
across that surface, on the ice of a white page
not only your breath
your name as well vanishes from the body
irretrievably.

7.

A model patient
in the corridors of the occiput, in the gray
of the sublime matter. Blind, deaf, without wants
on a gurney with wheels of wax
carted here into the depths
to the center of pain.
Model patient, motor in implosion
fragile pistons with minuscule, timid beats
in capillaries ready to erupt through the mycelium.
Purple, purple, purple.
Sack of words like blind, squirming mice.
Sack of gray lead.
Model patient. Any wants? No wants.
Yet the body flushes in a rash
of unspeaking lips.

8.

For so long had I believed this camel's back was the desert—
imagination inflating the flaccid lungs of the real
with brutality, with hallucinogenic shadows,
with fondest names, with superlatives.
The controlled effect of this abstract
weapon: my brain in explosion.

9.

Strangling lock
cloud sucked in straight to the kidneys
straight down to your final written breath.
Oxygen, oxygen, oxygen.
Abstract tubes abruptly snipped
with her silver shears.
Letters, letters.
Like the sun's rays on haystacks
like raw recruits on a train.
Mortal. Immortal.
Oxygen
oxygen
oxygen.

                              translated by A. J. S.

III. Lethal Dose

EACH POEM OF MINE

the ring where I'm down for the count
to your screams and taunts.

A. J. S. & D. C.

SEA-LEVEL ZERO

To know you are here, at this point, at sea-level zero of luck,
unable to do anything, promising everything, with the recklessness
    of a teenager,
now, in your forties, when your sole freedom is that
of remembering.
You've been in this hotel before, from exactly this same place you've
    stared out over the roofs,
the rain, the dust, the undulations of the walls.
With your tongue you collect the salty wetness from the corners of your
    mouth, you don't know when it was you cried,
you close your eyes but that doesn't solve anything, because you are
    here,
at sea-level zero of luck, lying to others and lying to yourself, spring will
    come.
But already it's gone, it took place yesterday, it lasted from three to
    three-thirty. No, that can't be true,
you're shouting, there's still time, I promise you, you're sobbing, in your
    arms you hug the pillow tight,
and with it, in the darkness of your room, the thousand women from
    your memory.
No, that can't be true, but yes, of course it is, the thousand happy days
    of your life
for which you can't find a suitable word.
"You can't find anything in this house," the woman shouts from
    the kitchen, "nobody
takes care of anything here," then the door slammed shut, the hail
    of words
which make you sick, you feel your heart tumbling in your chest,
    the air thinner and thinner,
a throbbing at the temples.
        . . . You'll get dressed and you'll leave. But not now.
Now, in slow motion, you're repairing the bathroom faucet,
you're watching your hands and then, only then, you remember

your double existence, with happiness, with humiliation, because
    everything has taken place before,
hasn't it? The journey through the mountains, in some other season,
    with some other woman beside you,
everything has taken place before, the tears, yes, and the knot in your
    throat, the explosion of the aorta. It doesn't mean anything.
Spring will come, you repeat to yourself, the same spring from
    twenty-five years ago,
from last year, because your sole freedom, here, at sea-level zero of luck,
is remembering.
The same as ten years ago, as last year, you'll get dressed and you'll
    leave.
But not now. Another time. Whenever. Someday.

A. J. S. & D. C.

TATTOOING

My nerves are silent
their blaze was once rosy.
Now it's gray.

Some time ago
I said with proud voluptuousness:
the body—my only heresy.
But all heresies come to an end
by acknowledging dogma
by finally making covenant with the consuming fire
until you cease to feel it.
My body has itself forgotten that frenetic conjugation
being, to be.

Its flesh
for such a long time has not been flesh
sacred letters are tattooed
all over its skin:
it is purely a sentence (with predicate impossible to find)
in my own mind.

A. J. S. & I. I.

THE BURNING

Hey, you, flesh that's mine,
I've fed you specially on magic embers!

I've placed bets on you with my high hopes a flop
for you never came in first
not in the trot
not in the routine races
to say nothing of the high-stakes gallop!

Your skin crinkles like paper now
our blood is as blue
as ink
soon enough we'll both of us take back
our illusion and mistake.
But what do you know in your fairy-tale manger
where you tremble submissively?—
what little you care!

So very soon my spirit
will overtake you
with its bare icy claw.

A. J. S. & I. I.

LESSER GEOGRAPHICAL DISCOVERIES

What a happy land
I could have been
what a happy land I used to be
what an America under Columbus's
heels—between nine and ten
between nine and ten in the evening
our geography lesson
gulf by gulf, valley by valley
with his hands drawn
on this bitter map.
Oh, the lesser
and the grand canyons of loneliness
overwhelmed by the cascading laughter
of a thousand Niagaras.
Between nine and ten
the geography lesson until he
showed up, the little demon from the north
from the far north
from the glaciers
the little demon of lucidity
a lantern in his left hand
who with his translucent right hand
cold like crystal
uprooted me and threw me out
cracking my head against the lintel:
which Columbus, what Columbus
this one between seven and nine in the morning
pretends to be Vasco da Gama
and discovers India
he is a professional of illusion
a charlatan, a temporary part-time instructor
sneered the little demon in disgust
taking refuge in his north
in the far north under the polar

ice cap
while his hands
a conquistador's
filled suddenly with all
the spices of an Indies morning
and Niagara plummeted
like a lead curtain
over our geography lesson
over the happy humiliated land
which I could have been, which
I was, which I am
today and tomorrow and tomorrow
and tomorrow.

A. J. S. & D. C.

MAINTENANCE MAN

Let him come and repair
what still can be repaired.
This frightened contraption
the crushed, stripped nerves, the scattered hardware
of hours and hours flung into a common
grave.
Let him come
and with his pump of illusion
inflate today all the way through tomorrow.
Which today, what tomorrow?
I inhabit an absolute
vacuum
where words
are the solitary living objects, sorry, painful
and fed to bursting with my own blood.
That blood he pours
into the pouch of the IV
at regularly scheduled intervals.
Let him come
the maintenance man
to put to rights
these squalls of tears
and this presumptuousness
which is poetry.
And as for me, let me watch in fascination
his skillful hands
the hands of a master mechanic
the same ones that could have caressed me
if he hadn't been devoting himself
every moment of every hour
to the towering guillotine of today
and tomorrow
if he hadn't polished it
to incandescence

if he hadn't forced me
to stay wordlessly beneath it
to describe
and contemplate it.

A. J. S. & D. C.

REPLAY

Something is rotten. rotten and glowing.
phosphorescence of wood decomposing.
the immaculate signs of the text
setting ablaze the white screen of the page.
and yet:
the words of my poem haven't loved
only one man.
here's a sentence which humiliates me.
replay, calls the director from his editing booth.
the tragic grace of the body in its descent.
its shattering.
a mannequin breathed life in our laboratories.
replay. postsynchronous:
my words haven't loved only one man.
between them and me
a no-man's-land I can't pass through and can't give a name to.

A. J. S.

CURTSY

Serenissimus, I beg you to forgive me for everything,
for the halo which I knotted around your neck
by force,
for the torrent of feelings
for the disagreeable task of looking up their meaning in dictionaries.
Forgiveness for dragging your peace-seeking self
through the golden dust of two printer's galleys.
And more:
I promise to forget how for one entire summer you filled
my transcendental attic with perfume and diamonds
with fiery ingots, with honey stalactites
my yard, my pantry, my retreats;
I promise to view you from now on as a rare stamp
posted on an envelope in transit to Atlantis.

A. J. S. & M.-A. T.

PITCH AND YAW

We'll never see the mountain. nor the sea.
loving this melancholy and salty circumstance
in it I recognize the blood. in it you recognize
the self-denominating word.
that too is a desperate way of matter's turning
wayward.

A. J. S.

FALSE PARADOX I

The deeper you are
in my being,
the more I long for you,
because you are without being—
like the heat of a flame, the swell
of an ocean wave,
like the sigil of death inscribed at the core
of the living cell.

I'm inhabited by you inescapably, like the believer
by the Holy Ghost,
to the marrow of the bone.
Not a fiber that is part of me
can deny your existence.
My spirit alone.

A. J. S. & D. C.

SLOPE

The mountains, the frozen tears and derision, the stalactite of salt
an image which I climb with claws and teeth
a retrieval—my cost analysis of weeping
my outlawed duplicate—this poem
scaled again and once again jagged, precipitous memory
you're going to fall I'm going to fall
my alpinist my darling.

A. J. S.

A DEFINITION OF LOSS

A definition of loss by absorption.
The sea swallows the shore
and its wave is of stone
and of earth.
My brain
much more than my body
embraces you
and you are of syllable and of word.
Only my eye lies in wait for you
its ray follows your scent
invents you
refashions you for the thousandth time
my blind eye that does not see
that does not see anything
outwardly.

A. J. S. & M. N.

THE FIRE

All of a sudden
I must switch on the searchlights
hunt for
the most powerful magnifying glass
crawl through the viscera
of this pyramid of words.
Slaughter in cold blood
this fabled animal
which no longer wants
to swallow me.
Set fire
to this exposed film
on which I continue to see
what is not what is not
what is not.
And in this same instant
renounce cohorts of pale periphrases
and synonyms
for solitude.

A. J. S. & D. C.

HOMEOPATHY

Like a homeopathic
medicine—
our imaginary tale
of love.
The more it dissolves
in memory,
the more it counteracts
the words that negate it,
restoring itself infinitely.

A. J. S. & D. C.

PROPOSITIONS ABOUT MYSELF

January has gone by, April too has gone.

Here's a sentence that means nothing.
I offer no more propositions about myself.
Halley's comet has now gone by, will not come again
for seventy-six years.
But in recent days some poets
began a new life—
from the third floor of an enormous apartment building
in a brightly lit city
from melancholy
from the aorta's crook—
a new life can be begun
from anything at hand.
But I don't have the courage.
I'm not yet fully prepared.
A few trifles: the pride of loving Ptolemy
instead of Copernicus,
the frenetic eels agitating the entrails
of this petrified river,
the imagination
its arras behind which Polonius lies dead.
A few trifles: dodges, delays, swindles
fascination, fear, as if
I were viewing my own brain.
Image:
On the bathroom mirror of a hotel
someone had scrawled in soap:
Par délicatesse
fais gaffe, faut pas
perdre la vie!

Under the violet fluorescent light, my face, for several seconds betraying the scars of those words.
But I no longer know their language.

A. J. S. & D. C.

LANDSCAPE WITH LIBRARY

The rain licks at the gingerbread roof of the world
wet mouse, this question mark
somewhere in a book, somewhere in another century.
it's raining in mocking gales of laughter over the black cloak
of Count Vronsky.
alone by myself, a double journey
in a library desolated by the rains
"my beloved, o my beloved"
arching above us, all the heavens.
and I—
I beat with my wet stick on the locked gate,
with my white stick I beat
on this book cover as on the wall
where I'm again sketching the window
that I can never open at all.

A. J. S. & D. C.

SEPTEMBER

September with gates of leaves like embers—
I pass through the raw wound of their emptiness,
beneath the dry ticktock of spasmodic rains,
a mime indifferent to somersaults and farce.

My arms enfold you—but only in my mind,
and my gesture seems to suggest incest.
Can you know how unnatural is this gesture,
born from me, conceived in my literature?

I'm drunk on you, like the vineyard on its grapes.
Forgive this vice, my everyday addiction
of delivering you in woe and passion.
For my poetry, Lord, let me be forgiven.

A. J. S. & D. C.

FALSE PARADOX II

Your existence
meticulously imagined by me
line by line by line
rests its foundations on the plane of the real
just as the indestructible pyramid
of words
on a derisory rectangle
of paper.

A. J. S. & D. C.

AN EXERCISE IN REMEMBERING

An exercise in remembering.
A vertiginous collapse backward.
Two years. Not even that.
Two short salvos.
The blindfold for the condemned. No.
The last request and the first. No.
The vowels of despair like water swirling in the throat.
33. Fragment from some
telephone number
or
the postal code on letters to the void.
Or the age of the triumphal death.
Two years back. Formless magnetic core,
darkness
in which tiny quartz crystals
wait in diabolical ambush.
Two short salvos. Two quick volleys of guffaws.
An exercise in remembering.
Geometric locus of
the most brightly glittering cruelty.

A. J. S. & D. C.

THAT'S ALL

Your heart alone,
I can still hear
from time to time.
Its frightened beat
like a bird with a single
wing.
That purple vein alone—
today it remains
etched into my retina.
Its curve
of an unknown letter
for whose perfection
unhurried death worked
with silver chisels.

A. J. S. & D. C.

WITHOUT EQUAL

I can no longer wait for you.
There's no more time.
I'll behave like a whore
when they appear,
the consummate cavaliers.
The sleep, the abyss,
the sublime darkness.
What passionate lovers
they will be. Without equal.
Without equal their embrace,
a perfect mixture
of ferocity and grace.

A. J. S. & D. C.

AN EYE GOING BLIND

I've forgotten your name. your smell and taste.
the greek serenity of your body.
the transcendent curve of your imperial torso.
I've been cured of you
as an eye going blind
gets cured of light
or the assault by an unearthly landscape.

A. J. S. & D. C.

THE HEMISPHERES OF MAGDEBURG

My flesh is getting bored.
your fingers are already tired.
soon we shall see the dentures, the Teflon parts,
the machinery of this supernatural state.
soon we shall be able to conjugate again, without trembling:
I am, you are
separate, separate.
our intact cells
will forget absolutely every clause,
our confused instincts will lay down
their muzzle
upon their dazed paws.
no, it's not the explosion stalking the ventricle that worries me
not the scarlet blaze of this state of mind
not the adrenaline shock that I fear
not this small flame here
ever smaller
but this love, hopelessly twinned
nearly incestuous
between our two occiputs thinking
the same word both at once.

A. J. S. & S. C.

HERESY

Really, I once had
such great potential.

Really, I diagrammed for him
the Bermuda Triangle
on just a few torrid inches.
Hey, you soul in a dog collar! Hey, flesh with ridges!
Hey, you dizzy blood bloated with birdshot!
He was prepared for soft drugs
for pygmy illusions. Not
for an extraterrestrial lady—
he'd never seen one. Never tried.
For him nobody had ever landed from the sky.

Really, rotting away at the tip of his collar,
I was his cyanide.

A. J. S. & S. C.

ABSENCE

No more poems. Only the vast echo of emptiness
deafening me—
on a screen of memory, your lips, voiceless,
trying to form a word.
I haven't the strength to decipher it.
Only desperate vowels rolling and rolling, meaningless—
invading my brain.
I don't even remember my name.
You used to have hundreds.
Because your hundred eyes once
reflected me, your hundred hands
once caressed me. I invented you so.
Between myself and me
this curtain of deafening silence.
No pains, no desires.
Only the motion of your lips
trying to give me a name,
to make me live.
The silent motion of your lips, saying something,
or perhaps simply kissing the void.

A. J. S. & D. C.

THE HUNGER

This cat is the one thing left after our breakup
(not counting children, telephone bills, losing lottery tickets, etc.).
Petting her in the darkness (just the two of us here),
I like to imagine her dilated pupils searching for a crumb of light,
for another stroke of my hand.
That night, yes, I had to be with him.
But no words. Only the waves of lava
and the absolute belief I was going to die.
I didn't. I married him, made him children, good food, boring days,
poems, a lot of trouble.
Everything, except something unnamed—
because, yes, I still remember my amazement
when the next day, he was chief accountant
and then a secretary watching over my glamorous career,
and later on a perfect brother.
I didn't know how to love the three of them.
What's wrong with this, could anyone say, anyone who knows
the true definition of a couple?—
an amulet, pleasing all others' sight,
a slogan, "the basic cell of our society,"
an efficient working device.
So what did you expect to be?
The guilt's within you yourself.
No, no, purrs the cat beneath my hand,
a couple is an entwined solitude.
You know it, she says—try to figure it out:
an imaginary tiger waiting for another imaginary beast.
Love
is the ferocious hunger between.

A. J. S. & D. C.

THE SIGNATURE OF LIGHTNING

Face to face, sitting here
in this room, in this jar of formaldehyde,
two speechless specimens in the museum
of our different memories.

Once I used to call him "Lord of My Tears."
Once I saw in his eyes (instead of my image)
colorful scenery, falcons and colts,
restless waves—and all the other synonyms
of desire.

Meanwhile I've covered the mirrors, I rid myself of the remains.
I grew old. I got cured, I think.

Before me now, a blind and tired bird in a cage.
Golden bars cutting his flesh, making him bleed.
I can no longer stand this image of him in my eyes.
To free him, I had to turn blind.

This image of us, sitting here,
doesn't even exist, except in God's eye. Because
more bitter than death is love.
This sentence could have been written by lightning
on the endless black sky, surrounding us
in this endless blink of our silence,
in this deserted museum
of our different memories.

This is not a love poem
but the trace of the lightning, burning my eyes,
though blind.

A. J. S. & D. C.

SPASM

On the lip of the precipice
between two blood vessels
between two words
through the eye with two apples from paradise you pass by me
in a barque of silver raising bitter sails
and I don't have and you don't have
any way to the sea.

A. J. S.

LETHAL DOSE

Now
no longer can I come
to any harm. I look at things
people and dogs—
all the water in the sea
that can't wash away the drop of blood I write with
the water he rinses his hands with
washing away everything that happens and most of all himself
serene, in his most natural way
he wants to scrub clean of the miracles
by which I still possess him today
at the core of those cells sick with fear
even in his words in the plasma there
crucified just as they are on an abstract cross
that I'm no longer strong enough to bear
to the summit of that very peak surmounting the heavens
on that hill on my knees as for alms
where there is no one to take away from me
the cup filled to the lip with the water
dripping from his palms.

A. J. S. & S. C.

IV. Seven Illusory Contours of America

A FAIRY TALE

That day in Iowa I remembered my grandfather's hands
rolling a cigarette on the porch.
It was the late '50s, after he came back
from deportation.
He was always silent, staring for hours into space.
None of us was more than twelve,
and we wanted to be *told*,
as if *that* could have been a fairy tale.
He never told us the fairy tale.
Later, I found out that he and my grandmother Ana
had been deported because they were considered
rich exploiters: they owned
two cows and a ewe.
Later, I heard from my mother
they were taken by train one night:
a wardrobe, some clothes, a clock, two shoes,
not a pair, because my grandfather had lost his right leg
during the first World War—a national hero,
like others who met again
after many years in the deportation camp
on the boundless Bărăgan Plain near the Danube,
where for four years he and my grandmother lived underground,
in their own wardrobe.
Now, looking across the fields
through my window, I try to imagine that plain where,
far from any city, my grandparents lived, digging and digging
a cave with their hands, their future home.
"The Americans will come to rescue us someday,"
my grandmother used to say, while
on Grandpa's face you couldn't see any expression.
Meanwhile Little Red Riding Hood turned out to be
the wolf, a greedy hungry one, meanwhile

it began to rain blood-red confetti.
The Americans did not come.

A. J. S. & D. C.

RETIREMENT BUILDING OR VANILLA DEATH

The beauty salon, the gym, the library—
the old frail fingers
turning the book pages: *Life After Life*,
caressing the huge cold terra-cotta cat
in the lobby,
picking up the last crumbs of cake.
Plastic flowers, aseptic corridors.
Pink and blue.
Pink and blue, pink and blue—
can you tell who's next? Guess who!
Death comes here in pastel colors
smelling of vanilla sugar and gingerbread.
"They must be rich, they must have
everything here," someone says.
I'm learning new meanings, new synonyms:
Eagle is no more a bird,
but a supermarket.
And
everything, sometimes, the end.

A. J. S. & D. C.

GRAMMAR

In front of the Retirement Building—
the national flag.
On Mr. John's balcony, in Allison's garden
surrounded by carrots and thyme,
above the White House, on the policeman's desk
the national flag.
In hospitals and stadiums, kindergartens and graveyards
every day, everywhere
living for it and dying for it
in Vietnam, Somalia, Kuwait
whether necessary or not.
A perpetual holiday, a memorial,
a sign of identity, a proof.
A continuous presence, a continuous present.
The *future in the past* is exclusively British.
The grammar of American life ignores it.
Sometimes, the lack of history
is a blessing.

A. J. S. & D. C.

THE STREETS OF PHILADELPHIA

The streets of Philadelphia,
different from in my imagination.
Altogether different. The suburbs—
Armenians who eat white cheese like in the Balkans,
children like in the movies or in film clips
on CNN.
A skyscraper of iridescent scales
like a trout launching into the sky.
Adam and Nancy
guiding me to the world-famous bell
with its crack.
And I, striving to translate into Romanian,
without success,
that cardinal point from the most democratic
declaration of principles in the world.
Trying to understand what it is to pursue happiness
simply because one must.

A. J. S. & D. C.

WESTERN PEOPLE, EASTERN CREATURES

This isn't the New World but another.
Love, death and life may be the same.
But the way you see them is different.
The chemistry of the cells, maybe.
Here everyone is allergic to something:
wind, dust, sun, water, mushrooms.
Everyone wary of bacteria, microbes, unknown new viruses,
as if a great disease were lurking around the corner.
Maybe here life is worth living. That's why they want to be immortal.
I know at least four immortal Romanian writers and painters
dead of hunger and cold,
of bitterness and despair, with unfinished poems
and paintings in their brains, reminding me
of that unforgettable image from childhood:
a split-open hen, with her necklace
of golden eggs, never laid.
We used to have other worries. Untranslatable.
A vast interior dread.
But it seems that the sum total of danger must be the same.
Here it's fashionable to be a nonsmoker, a vegetarian,
an allergic, a fragile being enjoying a favorite weakness,
growing it tenderly, loving it in the end.
On my desk, a panoramic view of Chicago,
a postcard already written. I just have to lick the stamp.
Bringing it close to my tongue, I think—
there could be a lot of bacteria.
This new feeling: a shortcut to madness
or a small step toward democracy?

A. J. S. & D. C.

NEW YORK, NY

Humble and pale on the streets of New York,
crushed by the endless shadows of the skyscrapers,
tattooed by the multicolored lights,
my eyes in pain, invaded by thousands of images.
After these many years, my many hopes and nightmares—
finally *here*, in this New World.
No pain no gain—a saying translatable into any language.
"Where are you from?"—the inevitable question,
its bitter edge, straight into my heart,
thrust in its core,
and my hands, suddenly trying to protect
the grenade full of tears, ready to blow up
into my throat.
"I am from the third world, from the fourth,
from the last possible one.
I am from nowhere. I am not."
"Come on, have fun. This is real—
not some movie.
And if it were, so what?
You aren't a main character. Try to act normal.
Don't tremble, please, above all don't cry.
You're not a main character, you're
not on stage,
you play no part in this scenario, you just won't do.
Be happy, have fun.
You'll forever be one of the extras."

A. J. S. & D. C.

HOMELESS

In another reality
far away from home, from your youth,
from your ever-stranger body,
far away from yourself.
In your window the autumn
sketches hieroglyphics
with its naked branches.
Trying to decipher the meaning, the code,
your eyes, full of tears, find none.
In another reality, which rejects you
with a tender, benign smile,
offering you in exchange this perpetual autumn
smelling of death.
And you, writing poems in another language,
feeling, for the first time, homeless.

A. J. S. & D. C.

V. The Writing Lesson

BREATH

My hand that writes
disappearing into the paper's whiteness, its cold, neutral
flesh, all the way past my shoulder, to the last
fluttering of my eyelid. a suicide—
elegant
just about letter perfect.

A. J. S. & S. C.

SCRIPTA

So I'm merely this
a word in the belly of another word.
sad nativity. shapeless agglomeration of lead
you've got no name. you'll never have any.
with ten sightless fingers the Compositor
gathers up breath, picks out blood, the pulse.
and you've got no name, placenta of lead
in which I dwell
with my knees drawn up to my mouth
with my nails plucking at my brain
you poisonous one, ash-gray Mary of tears
which I lend you freely that you may be:
abcdefg.

A. J. S. & I. I.

LET ME CONFESS

words' uselessness.
Their powerlessness
in face of the real.
The word *death*, as I was saying,
hasn't the ground
to put as much as a wrinkle
in the page it's written on.
Nonetheless
let me attempt to reconstruct your being
knowing all too well
that I can sketch your outline
only imprecisely,
and the word *life* will never
be able to fill it
with life.
Let me hold out,
lingering in the desert
of this tragic utopia,
superimposing thirst as an illusion
upon water as an illusion.
Exactly the singular opportunity
poetry gives me.

That is to say, again to establish
the hydraulic principle of communicating vessels
and to hear the slosh of words,
their liquid wandering
from one side of imagination
to the other,
from one irreality
to another.

A. J. S. & M.-A. T.

LOST POEM

"What have they done to my song, Ma?" You, they, all of you,
each one any way he could.
Take a sheet of paper and write. Reconstruct the poem.
At the Linnaeus Museum they reconstructed an animal
    from a phalange
and now rows of bored pupils stare at it.

There are animals and animals.
This wild beast will kill me.
This one is cast from a mold. This one gets stuffed with cotton.
This one doesn't exist.
She has ferocious maxillaries, she has syllables.
She will kill me. He . . .
This lost poem torn to pieces
inside a ridiculous taxi.
"What have they done to my song, Ma?"
Every last thing they could.

Like the runner of Marathon my soul staggers into the month
    of December.

I've forgotten, it says, striking against clenched teeth.
This is a sentence of victory.
Meanwhile I go on trying to reconstruct a poem
which I can't remember any part of.

Rejoice, I have won.

A. J. S. & M. N.

HARP OF BLOOD

How unnatural and pale this hand writing
it touches the things I once loved
fragments of time

your torso
on which my shadow draws hieroglyphics
obsessively.

Let's read them, let's read them
my blood cries out delirious
let's know what's there
let's explore that far
to the ultimate consequences so to speak

but the two of us—
this hand that writes and the written letter it made—
oh, how afraid we are.

A. J. S. & S. C.

THE EARTH

I believed I was
a word
turned upside down in His huge pupil
which forgave me
all my sins
His pupil which preserved and supported me
in His rays
in His ever wakeful eye.
I felt wholly sustained
when I could believe myself spelled out
by His great endurance
until I sensed
my animal must
until I saw rotting in the ground
the claws of stone
of the sad tiger of my being
and the living bone.

A. J. S. & D. C.

AQUARELLE

The blind finger before the typewriter
quick taps (vena cava—auricula dextra—via aorta).
A Cinderella picking lentils from cinders:
words from other words.

The blind man before an aquarelle—
black sky with anthracite sun.
Words—rats—flames—water monsters—toads.

The star fills up with me
and explodes.

A. J. S. & D. C.

ANAMORPHOSIS

Like a recruit in training, confused yet conscientious
I take everything with me. I leave everything behind. I don't know
whether the alarm is false, whether the war
really means war. I don't know how long I have left
to live. Under the searchlights, under the enemy's fusillade
I take out my tools and began to draw
not a display window not a pastry shop
not a necklace of neon light.
Like a recruit in training
befuddled and feverish
I take a pencil out of my pack
and I draw a wooden cross and my open left hand
which, using my right, I pierce with the iron spike
of these words.
Then the camp followers and the ball boys on the court
and those who don't believe in talent
the rockers who heave on their shoulders
the totality of these props,
all, every last one of them, though they know
I'm merely drawing,
crave to see blood where the spike drives through the flesh, real blood.
I'd like to, but I can't applaud
with my lone hand
murderous and sacred.

A. J. S. & D. C.

PASTEL

Summer in twilight, its calm and plenitude.
The soft asphalt where you leave delicate imprints,
the rosy air
which you're rowing through with folded wings,
somnolent, feeling free,
trying to remember, for your own sake,
a hill with apple trees from last autumn,
the swish of the scythe through the grass of the heavens.
And the heavens between the syllables
as through a net of leaves shimmering
in the August wind.
In the underground tunnels of the subway you run
with your pockets full of the afternoon's
hot coins.
You must pay for this cube of coolness,
this wait you'll have to pay for, your emergence at the surface.
In the underground tunnels of memory,
red and green lights,
images on which your words
glide helplessly: a hill with apple trees
from last autumn, a road lost
among the events overwhelming your retina,
while the train roars nearer and nearer
with its dark laugh,
while a tear like an auger
punctures the armor of the flesh
here and here and here.
It came, it passed by, it's all right now.
There's no one—a few masks,
as in a painting by Ensor.
Nothing, a few wrinkles under the makeup
between two stations, between two events:
miniature canals, unknown to mortals,
on the invisible face of the moon.

You must pay for this cube of coolness,
this wait you'll have to pay for,
your emergence at the surface.
The heavens through the syllables.
Here, down below, and there in memory.
A hill with apple trees, from last autumn.
And you, rowing through the rosy air
with folded wings, set free.
Trying to remember, for your own sake.
And here, here you are, an almost colorless ideogram,
a sentence printed in Braille.

A. J. S. & D. C.

A POSSIBLE TRINITY

In the rectangle of darkness
overwhelmed by joy, humiliation and servitude
belonging to matter,
a tenant in your own body,
endured by your own spirit . . .

Poetry, Illness and Love
a trinity which your blood devours
and resurrects with dour obstinacy.

Friday is an auspicious day, because then I arrived at the certainty
that nothing can happen *outside words*.
Their lukewarm flood invading the alveoli, the trachea,
filling my mouth, spurting through clenched teeth,
washing ceaselessly this rectangle of darkness
where day after day death signs its name
in an unknown language.

A. J. S. & D. C.

THE GOLDEN MEAN

Bellagio, Italy

Alone, surrounded by this scenery,
humiliated by its perfection.
The golden mean.
And this sheet of paper—empty and silent.
A cold rectangular iceberg.
A hot bittersweet raft, waiting for me,
poised to float, ready for my words.
But I'm not here.
I belong to the landscape
(a small stone, a leaf, a dusty piece of nothing)
added to its perfection, so close
to the perfection of death.
I'm not here.
From far away I watch
this blank sheet of paper, now overrun by ants.
Hundreds of them, restless,
rewriting this poem from the beginning.
Rewriting my life from the end.

A. J. S. & D. C.

THE LIONS OF BABYLON

One morning
five thousand years ago.
In the subcellars of stone
beneath the palace
to the left of the scribe and to his right
the lions of Babylon.
The scribe
has never seen the sun
has never seen the river
has never seen the sea.
Hunched over the clay tablet
he is now writing
about the sun.
He makes a minute description
of the flowing of the great river
into the sea.
The slave who dictates this to him
on his part too
has never seen the river,
the sun, the sea. He himself
heard about them
from yet another slave
who pressed the length of his body to the wall
until he gave up his breath
until he gave up his blood
until he received in his body
the light from beyond
the murmur of the river flowing
into the sea.

A. J. S. & D. C.

LAVA

All that I loved, I've killed.
Even the trajectory of your hands
inflaming my forgetful body
will enter from now on into a sentence
as a boy pharaoh into the icy cold of the pyramid.

All that I loved, I've killed.
Each verse—a sumptuous tomb,
the atrocious amber encasing
life,
the ravenous animal which licks
not my hand
but the Compositor's hand soiled with lead.

All that I loved, I've killed.
With the painstaking precision
of the taxidermist,
of the botanist affixing into the herbarium
the luminous corolla.
With the cruelty of a child
transfixed by torn-off butterfly wings.

I've nearly no time to live.
All the happenings that were mine—
plunged to the hilt into lead.
I'm the city of Pompeii
drowned deeper and deeper by the lava
of my words.

A. J. S. & D. C.

THE WRITING LESSON

I'll have to repeat the course.
The professor says:
Describe that waterfall
dazzling and majestic
in the sunrise.
I stand with eyes staring
at an anemic thread of water
trickling into the mouth of a drain
and I say in all humility, I can't
no, I can't.
You lack wings, the professor says
you lack the tiniest scrap of metaphysics.
Repeat after me now:
whiteness dazzle brilliance crystal
(ecstasy).
Whiteness dazzle perfumed words
in lace most neatly starched
through which with great impertinence
reality feverishly gushes
like blood through an antiseptic
bandage.
My concluding argument:
last summer on the beach
the last word of a drowned man
dragged upon the shore
was the very stream of water
rushing out from his lungs.
I saw it with my own eyes: no
immaculate petals no
wings of butterflies.
Blood and water seeping into sand.

You fail the exam and you'll have to repeat
the professor says and he pushes me into the emptiness

of the seventh floor of the school.
He pretends not to see.
I pretend not to die.

A. J. S. & M.-A. T.

NOTES

page 19. "Sunset Boulevard": Billy Wilder's classic film starred Gloria Swanson as Norma Desmond and also featured William Holden and Erich von Stroheim (Paramount, 1950).

page 26. "Classic Movies": There is a distant allegory behind this poem, based on a suggestion perhaps not readily apparent to an American reader: the notion of the average citizen as an extra or stuntman protecting the stardom of the dictator, Nicolae Ceauşescu, with his cult of personality. The Trabant was an East German car, the cheapest available, with a body of specially treated and strengthened resin and wool-fiber mixture like thick, stiffened paper and a weak, two-cylinder engine that spewed pollution. The three phrases, "*dorogaia moia*," "*mon amour*" and "*szerelmem*," all mean "my love" in Russian, French, and Hungarian respectively.

page 37. "Point of Convergence": The town of Amara, on a lake by the same name, a Romanian word which means "bitter" (hence the place-name, "Bitterburg"), is about halfway between Bucharest and the Black Sea. Crăsnaru associates this name etymologically with one term for "love" in Romanian, the word "*amor*," which derives directly from Latin.

page 47. "Hidden Heart": The various phrases: "*wie schön*," "how pretty" in German; "*tzuika aha, mamaligutza*," German-inflected Romanian for "*ţuica* [pronounced 'tsweeka,'] a distilled brandy, usually from plums] yes, a little *mămăligă* [essentially polenta, a characteristic Romanian dish]"; "*qu'ils sont gentils les roumains*," "how nice the Romanians are" in French; "*drug moi*," "my friend" in Russian. The poet's co-translator, looking for a yodel that would resonate in English, borrowed this one by transcribing it from the early country singer and guitarist Jimmie Rodgers in his 1930 recording with Louis Armstrong and Lil Hardin Armstrong, "Blue Yodel No. 9."

page 59. "Fairy Tale in Fragments": The German epigraph translates as "Oh, Hansel, what misfortune!" The Latin phrase, "*soror mea mors*," means "my sister death."

page 61. "The Raft of the *Medusa*": Domokos Szilágyi was a Hungarian-language poet of Romania who killed himself. The title refers to the huge, highly realistic and dramatic painting by Théodore Géricault depicting the foundering of the *Medusa* off the coast of West Africa; out of hundreds on the ship, only fifteen men, after thirteen days at sea, survived on a makeshift raft. The *Rondanini* (or *Milan*) *Pietà* is Leonardo da Vinci's last, unfinished work of sculpture.

page 73. "The Burning": A familiar creature in Romanian fairy tales is the poor, weak old horse that eats fire (in the form of live embers), quickly gains strength, and becomes both invincible and a magic aid for the protagonist. The horse usually speaks warnings and carries the protagonist as well.

page 78. "Replay" : The echo of *Hamlet* is intentional in both the Romanian original and the translation, the familiar line spoken by Marcellus, "Something is rotten in the state of Denmark," at the end of Act 1, scene 4.

page 86. "Propositions About Myself": The lines in French are modified from Rimbaud, "Chanson de la plus haute tour" ("Song of the Highest Tower"), the second of "Fêtes de la patience" ("Feasts of Patience"), which begins, "Oisive jeunesse, / A tout asservie, / Par délicatesse / J'ai perdu ma vie": "Lazy youth, / Enslaved to everything, / Through fastidiousness / I wasted my life." The poem changes this to a warning: "Through fastidiousness / watch out, don't / waste your life!"

page 95. "The Hemispheres of Magdeburg": The title alludes to the apparatus used in vacuum experiments by Otto von Guericke. This seventeenth-century scientist also invented a water barometer and became *bürgermeister* (mayor) of Magdeburg.

page 98. "The Hunger": The quote in the poem echoes a basic tenet of Marxist sociology, as in Friedrich Engels's description of "monogamous marriage" as "the cellular form of civilized society" in *The Origin of the Family, Private Property and the State.*

page 99. "The Signature of Lightning": The phrase, "more bitter than death is love," echoes Ecclesiastes 7:26, "And I find more bitter than death the woman, whose heart *is* snares and nets . . ."

page 105. "A Fairy Tale": The story is a true anecdote from Crăsnaru's own family. The usually whispered phrase, "the Americans will come," was a continuous refrain for almost two decades in Romania after World War II after the communist takeover. The Voice of America and Radio Free Europe urged resistance, and Allied airplanes dropped a confetti of slips of paper bearing such messages in order to encourage the population. We now know the Allies never intended to intervene militarily.

page 107. "Retirement Building or Vanilla Death": Because of widespread floods, for part of her residency at the Iowa International Writing Program in 1993, Crăsnaru and fellow residents were housed in the Walden Place retirement community, with its statuary of cats and dogs. The book, *Life After Life: The Investigation of a Phenomenon— Survival of Bodily Death*, is by Raymond A. Moody. Eagle is a midwestern supermarket chain.

page 118. "Lost Poem": A 1970 top-forty hit, "What Have They Done to My Song, Ma?" featured the singer Melanie and, in a more popular cover version, the New Seekers. In the original poem, the refrain appears directly in English, in somewhat different phrasing. The renowned Athenian runner Pheidippides, already weary from a 300-mile round-trip to Sparta, ran the twenty-five miles to Athens to deliver the news of victory over the Persians at the battle of Marathon and immediately fell dead.

ACKNOWLEDGMENTS

Grateful acknowledgment is made to the editors of the following journals, where a number of poems in this volume, often in somewhat different English versions, first appeared:

The Antigonish Review: "Efficiency, Ecstasy";

Apostrof: "Sunset Boulevard," "The Bullet," "Point of Convergence";

Arts & Letters: "The Painting," "Pastel," "Sea-Level Zero," "Propositions About Myself," "That's All";

Coastal Forest Review: "Aquarelle," "Landscape with Library";

Hawaii Pacific Review, "The Earth";

Kalliope: "Lava," "Eulogy for April," "After the Fall";

Litapalooza: "Western People, Eastern Creatures";

The MacGuffin: "Faun, Angel";

Mangrove: "Tattooing," "Fairy Tale in Fragments";

The Marlboro Review: "The Bullet," "July";

Metamorphoses: "The Perfect Eye";

Michigan Quarterly Review: "Classic Movies";

100 Words: "Pocket Survival Manual";

Oxygen: "Anamorphosis," "Maintenance Man," "The Raft of the *Medusa*," "Écorché";

Pennsylvania English: "The Monster";

Poetry: "Lethal Dose," "Breath" ©1991 The Modern Poetry Association;

The Poet's Attic: "The Earth," "Contest Image," "Letter to Nemo," "Pitch and Yaw";

Prairie Schooner: "Cheshire Cat," "Curtsy";

Press: "The Lions of Babylon," "The Signature of Lightning," "The Hunger";

Salt Hill: "The Last Day of Pompeii," "A Possible Trinity";

Tamaqua: "An Eye Going Blind";

Tampa Review: "The Golden Mean," "The Matchbox and Other Things";
Visions International: "Slope," "Scripta," "The Burning";
The Women's Review of Books: "An Exercise in Remembering," "Homeless."

Nine of the poems in this book—"A Definition of Loss," "Harp of Blood," "The Hemispheres of Magdeburg," "Heresy," "Lost Poem," "The Monster," "The Rehearsal Stage," "The Window in the Wall," "The Writing Lesson"—were included in *An Anthology of Romanian Women Poets*, ed. Adam J. Sorkin and Kurt W. Treptow, Classics of Romanian Literature, Vol. 7 (New York: East European Monographs with the Romanian Cultural Foundation Publishing House / Columbia University Press, 1994); 2nd ed., Romanian Civilization Studies, No. 8 (Iași: The Center for Romanian Studies, 1995).

Four poems—"Austerloo," "The Fire," "Indigo, Violet," "Lesser Geographical Discoveries"—were printed in *Leading Contemporary Poets: An International Anthology*, ed. Dasha Čulić Nisula (Kalamazoo: Poetry International, 1997).

What Have They Done to My Song, Ma? by Melanie Safka, copyright © 1970 by Jerry Leiber Music, Mike Stoller Music, Bienstock Publishing Co. All rights reserved. Used by permission.

Daniela Crăsnaru expresses gratitude to the University of Iowa International Writing Program, at which she was a fellow in the fall of 1993 under the sponsorship of the Coca-Cola Foundation and the University of Iowa, and to the Rockefeller Foundation, which provided a residency at the Foundation's Study Center in Bellagio, Italy, summer 1995, with additional assistance from the Roberto Celli Memorial Fund. Both grants supported work on these translations and the writing of a number of the poems that appear in this book.

Adam Sorkin likewise wishes to express appreciation to the Rockefeller Foundation for fostering the work on these translations with a residency at the Bellagio Center in parallel with Daniela Crăsnaru, as well as to Penn State University for its generous support through the College of Liberal

Arts Research and Graduate Studies Office, the Institute for the Arts and Humanistic Studies, the Office of International Programs, the Commonwealth Education System, the Center for Russian and East European Studies, the Delaware County Campus, and the Midwest Universities Consortium for International Activities (MUCIA). Also, work on this book was supported in part by grants from the Fulbright Scholar Program, with funding from the United States Information Agency, and from the International Research & Exchanges Board (IREX), with funds provided by the National Endowment for the Humanities and the United States Department of State which administers the Title VIII Program. None of these organizations is responsible for any views expressed. Sincere thanks to Thom Ward of BOA for his many helpful questions and suggestions. And finally, thanks to Nancy for careful reading, insightful criticism and advice, and just being there, as always.

ABOUT THE AUTHOR

Daniela Crăsnaru is one of Romania's major writers. *Sea-Level Zero* confirms her considerable talent. The author of eleven books of poetry and two collections of short fiction, she was honored in 1991 with the Romanian Academy Prize for career achievement in poetry, Romania's most prestigious literary award. Currently director at Ion Creangă, the country's leading publisher of children's books, Crăsnaru has been a force in Romanian politics since the fall of communism, and a leading advocate for free speech and human rights. She has also written three books of poetry for children. Crăsnaru's poems have been translated into French, Spanish, Italian, German, Greek, Hungarian, Turkish, Serbo-Croatian, Polish, Swedish, and Dutch. *Sea-Level Zero* is the first comprehensive American publication of her work.

ABOUT THE TRANSLATORS

Professor of English at Penn State Delaware County, **Adam J. Sorkin** is one of this country's leading translators of Romanian poetry. He has published eight previous collections of translations of Romanian poetry. Among them are *An Anthology of Romanian Women Poets*; *Transylvanian Voices: An Anthology of Contemporary Poets from Cluj-Napoca*; *The Sky Behind the Forest*, Liliana Ursu's poetry, with both Tess Gallagher and the poet herself; and the prize-winning *City of Dreams and Whispers: An Anthology of Contemporary Poets of Iaşi*. A former Fulbright Scholar and recipient of Rockefeller Foundation and IREX grants, Sorkin is a member of the American Literary Translators Association.

A celebrated literary translator, **Sergiu Celac** has translated novels from English and Russian into Romanian, including James Clavell's *Shōgun*. He has also translated Romanian poet Constanţa Buzea's work into English. Prominent in the realm of public affairs, Celac has served as Romania's Foreign Minister and Ambassador to the United Kingdom during the first half of this decade. He is on the National Council of the Romanian Writers' Union.

Ioana Ieronim is an important Romanian poet, editor, and translator. She is the author of seven volumes of poetry, as well as articles, reviews, and translations from English, French, German, and Swedish. Currently she is Program Director at the Fulbright Commission in Romania. In 2000, Bloodaxe Books will issue Ieronim's volume of narratively linked prose poems, *The Triumph of the Water Witch*, in a translation with Adam Sorkin.

Mia Nazarie is a poet, technical and literary translator, and now co-director of a private publishing house in Bucharest, Cezara Print, founded after the 1989 revolution. Her own poems and essays on poetics have appeared in Romanian literary magazines, and she has translated such disparate authors as Philip Larkin, Janet Frame, and Woody Allen into Romanian. Nazarie has also published a volume of poems for children.

Maria-Ana Tupan is a member of the University of Bucharest faculty, a literary editor, and an essayist whose most recent book is *Romanian Writers in the Universal Paradigm*. She has also written a critical study of the late Romanian Nobel nominee, the playwright and poet Marin Sorescu. Among her translations into Romanian are novels by William Dean Howells, William Gilmore Simms, Henry James, and Isaac Asimov.

BOA EDITIONS, LTD.
NEW AMERICAN TRANSLATIONS SERIES